TAKE THE PLUNGE

Become professional.

Graeme Smith

PUBLISHED ON AMAZON.com
by
LABYRINTH BOOKS

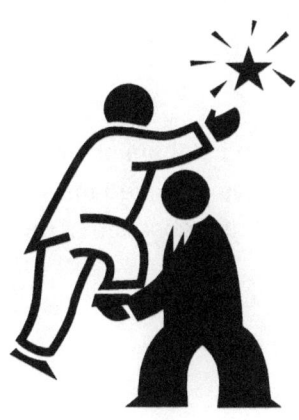

DEDICATION:

This book is dedicated to my family.

Hele-ly (Ly).
        my wife:

Ingrid.
        our daughter:

Marie.
        my former wife:

Fiona, Natalie and Michael
        our children:

Georgie
        Michael's wife:

Pearl, Kiki and Martha.
        their children:

They have had to put up with me for many years and I thank them for that.
I hope this book gives them an insight into what has occupied me.
All have done worthwhile and interesting things in the absence of my help.
I congratulate them for their achievements.

HOW TO USE THIS BOOK.

First think - then do.
Usually people don't think through things to the level they need to.
Because of that, they have projects instead of tasks on their "to do" list.
That leads to procrastination as it hasn't been broken down to a task level.

So go through your book once to understand it.
Go through it again.

Then start at the idea you would like to implement first.
Make notes of the steps you will need to take and the resources required.
Use these notes to create a step by step system for implementing the guide.
Often you will not refer to the original, once you've created **YOUR** system.

The first question to ask and answer is "Why is this being done?"
How does this align with where you want to get to?
What are the strategic implications of doing this?
Does this fit with getting to your goal in the shortest and fastest time?
What would it be like if it were totally successful?
Define it - what is success for this project and how will you know?

Now brainstorm all the tasks that are involved in your project.
It's important not to go linear too fast with this.
By linear, I mean step one, step two, step three, and step four.
You end up cutting off options.
As you plan step one, two, three, there is a specific step that might be four.
Start steps too quickly, other ways for one, two and three may not appear.

The first third of any brainstorming session is really easy.
Just come up with lots of ideas.
The second third is challenging - go through ideas and see where they lead.
Then push yourself to think a little bit outside the box.
That's often where the big idea is!
That's where the most powerful way of getting a project done fastest - is.

Most people never get to that level and short-change themselves.
Then their project takes longer and they also set up to procrastinate.
This final brainstorming part of the equation is incredibly important.

Once fully brainstormed put your options into a linear sequence.
Then you can figure out what you've overlooked.
Everything becomes obvious as you get your tasks in order.
Now add missing steps and you have laid out your task list for this project.

When you've organized the tasks into a linear process decide:
What things can you start immediately?
What can be started that are not dependent on what occurred before them?
Obviously that is step one.
There might be step five, six or twenty that don't rely on anything else to do.
You can get started on them right away too.

Now use a folder.
Write things you think of at the time and also cross off things as you do them.
Add in stuff that is relevant from time to time.

INDEX: TAKE THE PLUNGE!

SUPPORT:
Clipping Path Universe – for photo-shop editing

The International Artist magazine – international magazine for artists

The Australian Artist magazine – magazine for Australian artists

Cherri Computers – for computer hardware, software and printers

1. Why start small?

Reviewed by John Newell - (Ontario, Canada)
1. My mission is to help you make money as a professional artist.
2. Just imagine how many works an artist does in a year.
3. Will you do what everyone else does?
4. You should make money from your art.

1. My mission is to help you make money as a professional artist.

OK you can paint well.
You must believe that to even think about a professional career.
But you can paint very well and do it as a rewarding past-time.

In spite of a widely held belief your artwork doesn't sell itself.
If it did, you'd be able to hang your work up anywhere and people would buy.
You should know better than that.

You've done your apprenticeship.
You know how to manage time.
You also know how to be productive.
In other words make the best use of whatever time you have available.
You've learnt how to sell.
But that's not all you know!
You have a contact list of potential and actual buyers.
You've created a simple website as a way to help develop your contact list.
You also understand pricing and know the importance of framing.

With all that in place your career foundation has been laid!
Now you are ready for a professional career.
Will you do what everyone else does?
I can help you in a way you would never have previously believed possible.
BUT if you do **NOT** have **ALL** those preliminary steps in place.
Your career will **NOT** be as successful as you would like.
For example improved exhibition sales will probably **NOT** happen.
Your income will **NOT** compound as your prices rise with additional sales.
And you'll get very few referrals to increase the works you can sell.
There will be stagnation or even a decline!
You may even have experienced good sales in the past.
That doesn't mean they'll continue as the world has changed.
There is less discretionary income, so new things need to be done.
The number of works other artists do affects your place in the art market.

2. How many works does an artist do in a year?

I guess it's a bit like saying, how long is a piece of string.
Some artists create a few works, others hundreds and some thousands.
Printmakers, due to their chosen process, create more than most artists.
Don't distinguish 'good' from 'bad' artists, or realist and contemporary artists.
Just how many works are produced?

How many artists are there who paint, print or make other artworks?
Don't distinguishing 'good' from 'bad', or realist and contemporary artists!
I've seen figures suggesting 40,000 in an Australia Council report.
So just how many works are produced?
There are a lot of people working at producing artworks in your country?
But then there's the rest of the world too!

Now imagine you could look into each artist's studio.
A corner of a garage, spare bedroom, or elaborate purpose built structure.
While there, count the number of finished paintings, prints or other artworks.
Add on the artworks you see in all galleries and places where people buy art.
Don't forget works that are not on show but in the stockroom out the back.
Again we don't know how many this would be, except another huge amount.

How many artworks do you suppose are sold annually?
No doubt galleries sell quite a lot, as do many art shows.
Paintings are even sold over the fence to the lady next door.
No matter how sold, or for what amount, it's quite a large number too.

Total all works produced in a year by all artists and subtract those sold.
If the answer is a negative amount, then demand exceeds supply.
If the answer is positive, then supply exceeds demand.

It's pretty obvious that in the art world supply exceeds demand.
Unsold work, in studios, galleries etc. show supply exceeds demand.
Any industry where supply exceeds demand is a depressed industry.
This is true for the art industry as for the wool, car, housing, or any segment.

Know and understand this as a realistic step to what is possible.
If you wish to be a serious participant in the art industry, as an artist.
It's not usually sufficient that you be a 'good' artist.
Many very talented people do not 'make it' but others do of course.

What's the difference between the successful and those who are not?
It's not about becoming a 'good' artist!
You need intelligent planning, some courage, determination and persistence.

3. Will you do what everyone else does?

In real estate a buyer is told of one of the following circumstances:
The seller was going through a marriage break-up.
Or they were in a bit of financial trouble at the moment.
Or they had bought another house and were desperate to sell.
What's more, the seller would take a significant reduction in the asking price!
This is the standard approach to selling real estate these days.
It is because it works as sales people are generally quite pragmatic.
If you are buying and the seller is in one of these unfortunate situations.
It explains why there may be price reductions.

In these circumstances a buyer is more likely to make an offer.
But not if the house is on a 'take it or leave it' basis and that's why it is done.
To get the buyer to make an offer.
Once the buyer has made an offer, they've also made a commitment to buy.
That's if the price is right but selling is now a little easier.
Now it's just a matter of finding the right price.
That will usually be somewhere between that asked and that offered.
A potential buyer thinks a real estate agent acts in his interest.
It really is standard salesmanship.

You know of many instances of professional standards in our industry.
But some standards may even be misguided.
Many artists will not lower their prices because of loyalty to past buyers.
Even though this may cost them a sale right now.
And those buyers show no loyalty to the artist!

The professional standard you show is likely to be the one you receive.
I follow ethical standards dealings with others and expect this from them too.
No doubt you do the same.
Then there are artistic standards!
This has little to do with professional standards, but to what is 'good' art.

This is an artistic question rather than a professional one.
My focus is on helping you as a professional, market what you do.
The house-buying scenario was not to focus on ethics, or sales practices.
I imagine their conversations with vendors would be quite different.
But the main point is all real estate people use much the same approach.
In other words it's standard industry practice.

It's good having a range of practices that everyone follows.
We don't have to think (nor do real estate people) when we do those things.

They've been tested by time and everyone knows they'll work.
Traditions are standard practices, but time has passed, decades or centuries.
Passing time, nurturing traditions or standard practices, is a major problem.
Ways of doing things, which were appropriate at a certain time, change.
Many are no longer suitable or even necessary at a later date.
We no longer need to know how to mix pigment and binders to make paint.
We buy tubes of paint of better quality than 'old masters' could make.

Traditions may change over time, with later followers not realizing this.
Like the party game where a message is whispered to the next person.
They pass it on to the next, on so forth.
The message that returns to the originator is usually quite different.

Standard practices also apply to how you sell or market your work.
If you wish to sell, take your 'artist' hat off and put your 'professional' hat on.
The focus of this program is on the business and marketing side of art.
You can be a traditional artist and an up to the minute marketer.
But understand the two aspects can be seen as distinct and separate.
As a marketer or seller you cannot do whatever you like!
You are seeking to understand and influence other people's behaviour.
For professional success it's essential to be up with marketing and selling.
This doesn't mean do it yourself for that's why there are galleries and agents.

Galleries and agents are business people and so generally pragmatic.
In certain circumstances a new artist is likely to be invited to join their team.
Your first task is to find out what those circumstances are.
Then you can work out how to get the gallery to make you an offer.
Once they have made an offer, they've also made a commitment.
It's now a matter of finding the right arrangements.
That will be somewhere between what you'd like and what is offered.

4. You should make money from your art.

A visitor to my home saw a painting that he really liked.
He asked how much it was so I named a figure and a sale was made.
What he actually bought was my palette.

Your income is the ONLY objective way to measure your success.
Reputation, grants, fame, being in an art establishment, can't be measured.
So I do not concern myself with them.
I consider making money from art an honorable and worthwhile thing to do.
I reject the notion that receiving money will somehow diminish your art.

Selling is helping people buy.
There's no way to start a successful money-making career overnight.
You can't skip the fundamental steps needed for a professional career.
I assume you've done the work necessary to get your career off the ground.
There **IS** an easy way to a money-making career without breaking the bank.
Even better, you are almost there **BUT** it did take a while didn't it?
The easy way is to do things right the first time!

There is no ONE right way but there ARE lots of wrong ways.
If you get it right at the start your career path will open up.
Cut corners and it is **10x** harder in the long run but all is not lost.
It just takes longer **AND** you will learn a great deal from the wrong ways.
That includes why they are wrong.
If you do it right, you can't do all at once so there's **NO** success short cut.

Success is related to time and time has an effect on whatever we do.
If we've learned something we can build on it in ways not previously possible.
But we have to start with that initial learning.
Then relatively small ideas can become altered and improved.
That happens when the context changes or are associated with other ideas.

Most people have heard of the downward spiral or vicious circle.
On the other hand there is a matching upward spiral too.
Things start in a small and insignificant way.
Gradually they build and increase in momentum.

What happens when ideas link with other ideas?
Ideas can thus spiral upwards, so that they almost seem to be self-sufficient.
This upwards spiral is integral to the creative process.

The upward spiral also provides momentum that leads to success?
What if you learn how to focus on maintaining that momentum?
Then you can be ever more successful.
Even with small steps that attitude will lead to success.
Can spirals be powerful?
They seem to fuel themselves and become self-propelling in time.
Successful people get more opportunities to be even more successful.
Those who need opportunities never seem to get one!
Many people think this is luck, either good or bad depending on its nature.

Can we make our own luck?
Good ideas can come from anywhere.
It's up to you to notice and be open to them.
You also need to harness them to your advantage.

Will this momentum accompany a rejuvenated career?
Change will build slowly at first but gradually gain momentum.
Other spirals interlock and momentum gathers more rapidly.
In time success is attained once more but there is no short cut.

2. Foundation for expansion.
Reviewed by John Hill - (Chichester, United Kingdom)
1. Your career foundation has been built.
2. What do you want to achieve in your art career?
3. Does having a focus guarantee success?
4. Your focus is your future!
5. You should develop a long term focus?

1. Your career foundation has been built.

You can paint well and you've done your apprenticeship.
You know how to manage time and you also know how to be productive.
In other words make the best use of whatever time you have available.
You've learnt how to sell.

But that's not all you know!
You have a contact list of potential and actual buyers.
You've created a simple website as a way to help develop your contact list.
You also understand pricing and know the importance of framing.

BUT if you DON'T have ALL those preliminary steps in place.
Your career will NOT be as successful as you would like.
For example improved exhibition sales will probably **NOT** happen.
Your income will fall along with your prices with few sales.
There will be very few referrals to increase the number of works you can sell.
There will be stagnation or even a decline!

You may even have experienced good sales in the past.
However that doesn't mean they will continue now!
The world has changed in the last few years.
There is less discretionary income available so new things need to be done.

In spite of a widely held belief your artwork doesn't sell itself.
If it did, you'd be able to hang your work up anywhere and people would buy.
Without people willing to buy there will be no sales!

Past buyers can be leveraged into major career momentum.
They can launch a continued successful and sustained art career.
Ideally any exhibition builds on those that have gone before.
Successive exhibitions should generate progressively higher income.
That's why you should get the first one right.
Money from improved exhibiting techniques adds to money you now earn!

But not all galleries can do this for most do not know what to do.
If you seek a new outlet for your work you must assume this is the case.
That means someone else has to do it but where do you get the time from?
A lot of day to day stuff needs doing in any profession, including that of artist.
The more successful you are the more of it there is.
Meet people, phone calls, enter competitions, framing, handle finances, etc.
If you are successful you may even need an agent so there is time to paint.

2. What do you want to achieve in your art career?

A focus is the bridge that takes you from to-day to to-morrow.
Now you just paint, but in the future you see yourself selling many paintings.
This focus means you need a strategy for achieving that objective.
You can make such a change possible, and even profitable.
Just say this is what I am going to do from now on – then do it!
To the next level of your career from what you do today.
But you must make sure you have the right focus to get there.
You might say "I'm a local artist," thinking that is your focus.
But you have a theme that covers everything - just a set of words.

It is possible to develop a set of words to fit any scenario.
This theme might only mean you live in a particular place.
But you work in a range of mediums, cover different styles, etc.
The only local component is where you live and there's no focus in that!

All-encompassing concepts are the opposite of focus.
A broad concept covers more and more so it becomes more abstract.
It actually means less in terms of focus.

It would be different if you only painted local subjects.
Made materials locally, sold locally, localness is emphasized in what is done.
So focus is about less rather than more.
By its nature a focus doesn't cover everything you might do.
But is a way of pointing to the future.

At any time you should have three types of products,
Yesterday's products.
Today's products - which should be producing the bulk of your income.
To-morrow's products - which are your future.
There's what you focus on, what you sell, and what you will make money on.
They might be different things which could mean three different outlets.

A focus can and should change as circumstances change.
Nothing stays the same long enough for you to stay singularly focused.
The objective of your focus should be to lead you in a coherent direction.
If you want to be represented by a gallery then your focus should be clear.
You should be moving in that direction.
In addition your focus will tell them if you fit into their organization or not.

3. Does having a focus guarantee success?

It almost certainly doesn't provide that guarantee, not straight away.
In the short term, narrowing your focus may even cost you opportunities.
You sell off old stock cheaply, or abandon some services, say teaching.
You'll turn away chances that do not fit into your plans too.
Your local gallery wants your watercolours but you are only painting oils now.
Because oils are your focus you turn down this opportunity and lose sales.

A powerful focus is almost never effective in the short term.
If this were not true then every business would be enormously successful.
All you would need to do is try a number of different approaches.
What works, keep doing it, or replace what doesn't work with something else.
Sooner or later you establish a successful business or in your case career.

What works in the short term doesn't tend to work in the long term.
A business chasing immediate success, is ultimately headed for failure.
You need courage to make a focusing decision and wait for a market to react.
It won't happen overnight, but it will happen you just have to be patient.
Put another way, persistence is the key to success.
Make the correct decision and then keep moving forward with it.
At first progress will be slight, but momentum gathers, like steering a ship.
Initially it takes a great deal of effort to turn and little headway is made.
However, once pointed in the right direction, speed can gather.
Eventually only small inputs of power are required to maintain top speed.

I have likened a focus to energy, as a laser to light.
Concentrated light is extremely powerful and does things diffused light can't.
It's the same for another power source, your energy.
Focus your energy and you'll achieve what others consider impossible.
For once it's easier for an artist than a large business.
There's a danger with a big organization that any focus is lost in the crowd.
Committees can't find simple ideas, only complex ones.
But a focus is always simple - just think about the idea and then decide.

A focus for an artist is to be a good oil painter (pastel artist, whatever).
The more specific your focus the more you'll become like the laser.
What sort of things you paint, how much they sell for, how long it takes, etc.?
Then achieve this laser-like artistic goal in a series of small steps.
Large steps are daunting and you'll probably not get there.
What is your focus - you know you want to be represented by a gallery.

That means you can identify anything you do that doesn't fit that focus.
Eliminate those things.
When you have a focus, like the laser, you create a powerful perception.
A perception of value relates to your focus and is in a client or gallery's mind.

4. Your focus is your future!

Day to day activities should be secondary to your future goals.
You do have to do those but they are not so important.
Otherwise your hopes and aspirations are being left to chance.
Your primary task as an artist is to work towards future goals so they happen.
Predict your future and take specific steps to make it happen!
Many years ago, Volvo selected 'safety' as a focus.
They made a prediction about their future and direction of the industry.
They also decided how their present (then) activities would be carried out.

Deciding about where you want to head is not just wishful thinking.
Look at what you are doing to-day.
That single service, product, or idea is your best hope for the future?
It's that simple but it's also hard.
The hard part is making the right selection in the first place.
It's hard for you won't know you've been right until a lot of time has elapsed.
By then it's probably too late to return to one of the other gallery options.
Never-the-less this is what you must do.
Such a decision can have short term penalties!
But the longer you keep your focus the less important they will be.
You'll be increasingly sought out for what you are focused on.
You will also develop your identity at the same time!
Focus is a characteristic of winners so don't be sidetracked stay your path.

As time passes an upward spiral supports the original decision.
Your focus allows you to develop in ways not previously possible or foreseen.
A common scenario concerns which media should you use.
Early in a career you want to use many as all are exciting to explore.
This is a learning or student phase and is important.
Eventually you make a professional decision of the medium as your specialty.
It doesn't really matter, just so long as you enjoy it.
By spending more time with this particular material you'll get to know more.
You can do more, than those who divide their time using different materials.
The same kinds of comments apply to subject or style specialization too.

This doesn't mean you can't change your focus from time to time.
You can, but only if your goals are first changed.
These are only changed for something better (you achieve your initial plans).
Set sights high to start with - now more realistic but still in the same direction.

5. You should develop a long term focus?

A focus should be simple.
Then you'll keep on your pathway and won't be easily sidetracked.
If it's simple it's expressed in simple words and immediately understandable.
It can be shared with clients, employees if you have any, and the media, too!

You can't make yourself successful, only your clients can do that!
That's why your work needs to be at the best gallery.
They have the best and probably also the most clients!
If your focus is memorable it will be easier for their clients to remember you!
So what makes a memorable idea?
One important aspect is uniqueness at the time you first claim the focus.
What you say about yourself has to be different from what other artists say.
Audacity, even shock, can help make a focus memorable.
The more often it is repeated the more powerful your focus becomes!
The same is true of publicity but those ads that get repeated – work!

It's really about momentum.
It's the belief in your client's mind that you will be a great success.
Your gallery has to believe this too and then they can make it happen.
An upward spiral of dominance can result.
The more often the focus is repeated, the stronger it becomes.
Repetition is a powerful force and gives you the ability to control direction.

A good gallery's focus is powerful because it attracts the right clients.
Diversification comes with a price.
That gallery will lose focus and lose power.
Particularly against opposition that has retained its focus.
They'd be better with an increased share of business they already have.
That way they'll increase their power.
It's easier to increase a share in a business you know, than one you don't!

People knowing their own industry feel they can't make more progress.
On the other hand they're confident about what they don't know.
Unfamiliarity breeds a contempt, and puts them right out of a core business.
Think twice before you open a gallery or introduce work in another medium.

A focus should be revolutionary.
It's like pruning a plant, if you do it, you have a better and healthier plant!
Ask if a given decision will improve business focus instead of the bottom line?
But a narrower product line will mean lower returns, initially.
However ultimately there'll be an increase in market share.

The ultimate goal should be the health of your career.
A healthy career is narrowly focused with dominant market share, and profits.
It is almost impervious to competition.
Decide your focus and prune it of most things that don't fit.
Your gallery should fit as well, otherwise look for one that does.

Business should have long-term strategic plans and short-term goals.
A five to ten year time scale is enough for most businesses, including yours.
This gives you sufficient time to achieve something really major.
But prevents it from becoming too daunting in the short term.
Short term planning should deal with achievable objectives.
They carry you towards those longer-term ambitions.
You might want to be represented by a gallery to assist long-term ambitions.
For example you want to have a series of sell out exhibitions.

They're like signposts along the road to your destination.
You can tick them off as you make progress.
Eventually the destination comes into closer focus.
It follows short-term objectives are more precise than longer term ones.

3. Gallery representation.

Reviewed by Vincent Miller - (Scottsdale, Arizona)
1. Where will you exhibit?
2. The difference is professionalism.
3. Take back responsibility.

1. Where will you exhibit?

There are only two types of galleries.
Those who will take your work and those who won't.
You don't need the first as they are desperate and not successful.
They will go out of business usually suddenly.
The owner is probably honest and well-intentioned but has no money.
They can't promote without money.
Often they're thought to be "arty", but they really don't know what to do.

The other gallery owners don't need you – YET!
They're **NOT** looking for new artists their loyalty is to artists they represent.
These galleries have usually been around for some time too.
Their sales techniques are well honed and work.
They have a focus and seek clients who are interested in that focus.

Think about where you would like your first exhibition to take place.
Start from the top and pick the very best, most suitable gallery you think of.
It should be in a city not too far from you and sell works roughly like yours.
There should be a certain amount of prestige involved too.

Once you've decided on your gallery start getting used to the idea.
If your groundwork is properly laid, you'll go well as they're in business.
You **CAN** enter their artist ranks if you present a business opportunity.
What if your chosen gallery is reasonably distant?
You might start there but more likely is where you go for exhibition two.

But DON'T approach them as an artist.
Visit your chosen gallery as a potential buyer.
Ask the questions someone interested in buying works like yours might ask.
Do not worry about whether they will want to exhibit your work or not.
A little further down the track you'll need to – but not yet.

How will you get into that gallery then?
YOU will need to stand out from **ALL** other artists seeking representation.

A major gallery is a magnet for aspiring artists.
Every day the gallery (you want) is approached by one or more artists.
Gallery strategies for **NOT** adding more artists to their ranks are well-honed.

Your works do NOT need to stand out but the gallery approach does
What if your works are different from others the gallery has?
You will stand out but with few clients **AND** little interest from the gallery!
What do most other artists do?
They make an appointment to see the gallery owner/manager.
They have a portfolio with works the gallery person could be interested in.
They have documentation to demonstrate their achievements and ambitions.
They do not leave a stone unturned to be represented by that gallery.

They will fail - all of them.
You do not want to join their ranks.
So your approach MUST be different if it is to be successful!
That means **NO** portfolio.
NO documentation.
NO talking to the owner/manager.
Do nothing that all the other hopeful artists do.

But you need to visit the gallery for that's how you can find out things.
But visit as a prospective client and find out what happens to them.
Attend a social function or two (as a client).
Watch how the gallery people function.
Talk to some of the other people present and find out why they are there.
Ideally you might meet some who like works such as yours.
Find out why they like this gallery so you might meet some artists.
Talk to them about the gallery and also arrange to visit some at their studio.

Richard Bruland is an established artist in Los Angeles (USA).
So he has access to collectors of his works.
He asked one if he knew galleries in an area he was interested in exhibiting.

You may not have this type of contact yet.
But when you do use them in a similar manner.
You need to find such people who buy from the gallery of your choice.
The artists you met at a social function can introduce you or provide referrals.
This process will take some time so you have to be patient.

You must follow up those referrals or introductions.
Ask if you could meet them to show a few works.
Then tell them you'd like to be represented by the gallery of your choice.

You want their opinion about what you should do.
Do **NOT** try to sell your works to these contacts.
Do what they suggest as at least one will contact the gallery about your work.
They will recommend that the gallery of your choice has a look at your work.

This is the very best type of introduction you could have!
The recommendation is from a valued client.
The gallery will contact you and make an appointment to see your work.
There are others who could make overtures to the gallery on your behalf.
If an intermediary is favourably known to a gallery you are ahead.
Start thinking about who such people could be.
What about the artists you met at the social functions?
They might even pick up the phone and call the gallery.
They could tell the gallery they would bring you over so they could meet you.
Using clients or other artists for introductions will take time.
It won't be set up in an hour or two but you will get into the gallery.
And that will pay for any time lost.

As mentioned your approach MUST be different to be successful!
So what do you do?

Do the opposite of the one used for direct marketing.
This approach is characterized by multiple sellers selling at the highest price.
From the sales payments are made to others further up the marketing chain.
Each level is responsible for those who are on the next level below.
They get money from all levels underneath.
BUT they make payments to the next level above.

The person at the top gets money from all levels underneath.
They make the most money.
Those at the bottom make the least.
They just get paid for what they sell!

YOUR marketing approach starts small.
Contact anyone you know who might be able to help you (get into a gallery).
Ask them to contact people **THEY** know who might be able to help you.
Then suggest to your contacts what they could do next (to help you).
You suggest what they could tell (even do) their contacts to help you more.
Eventually you suggest their contacts approach the gallery on your behalf.
Then you receive a call from the gallery to discuss holding an exhibition!

2. The difference is professionalism.

Does being a professional artist mean you have sold some paintings?
Does it mean you can give up your regular job and live from your art sales?
For most artists being a professional tends to be one of these alternatives.
There should be some relationship between success and professionalism.
Success is defined in terms of goals you set.
Your goals may be creative, economic or whatever you choose.
To be successful you must achieve, or move towards achieving, those goals.
Put simply, if you have no goals you cannot possibly be successful.

Professionalism is about the way you achieve those goals.
It's about whether you actually set goals in the first place.
It is about checking progress along the way as you realize your ambition.
You give yourself the best shot and take opportunities as they arise.
It's **NOT** about compromise, unless it moves you to the predetermined goals.

Professionalism is an attitude towards what you are doing.
Professionalism is not the same as amateurism, or practicing a hobby.
These are worthwhile, but different forms of behaviour.
Just think about the professional tennis player.
They use the same racquets, balls, courts, and rules, as the amateur player.
BUT it's **NOT JUST** about being better.
It's **NOT JUST** about earning considerably more money either.
Although that is certainly how professionalism is measured.

A professional tennis player has to be outstanding to earn anything!
Not only do they set goals, they are often long term ones.
Planning is meticulous, takes account of their own ability and opponents too.
They practice far more than any amateur could or would.
There's a constant refinement of their game.
Professionalism in any field is an attitude towards what you are doing.

A difference between successful artists and others is professionalism.
It's definitely not talent for there are many talented but unsuccessful artists.
The same people also lack the professional attitude.
Are you a professional?
Will you approach your target gallery professionally then?

BUT using other people can save lots of time!
Olympic athletes must constantly reach new levels of achievement.
So sometimes they just have to do things that previously seemed impossible.
To get to Olympic level these days, you just can't do it on raw talent!

But you can't do it on your own either!
One sportsman has a strength coach, sports management person, a sports scientist, a fiancée, a coach and a secretary on his personal team.
Another has a team comprising, mother, coach, sports psychologist, teacher, nutritionist, doctor, physiotherapist, sponsor, coach (2nd one), masseuse, sponsor (2nd one), and sport manager.
Neither is in a team sport and most others have similar back-up teams.

The support team can provide a winning edge at the highest levels.
The difference between competitors is very small but can be magnified.
The support base and how hard the athlete trains are the magnifiers.
No person will win a gold medal on talent alone and in art it's the same!
Yes you may say, but there's money in sport and not much in art!
True, but it's not long ago there was no more money in sport than art.
In the sport set up, often it's the sponsor that's the money.
At least one of their support team has the job of obtaining sponsorship.
This can be done in art and probably has so you have someone do it for you!
Sponsorship money lets you to put together a support team for your career.

But to improve at anything is easiest at the beginning.
The better you get, the harder it is to lift the bar even a little higher.
That's why outside support is more likely for elite artists, like elite athletes!
In sport a support team can't make an average athlete into an Olympian.
The individual still has to do the work!

Just imagine what you could do with support like this?
There could be a drawing coach, a colour coordinator, and a paint supplier.
In addition you'd need an agent, art psychologist and a sponsor (or two).
Also framer, exhibition coordinator, business manager, and painting packer.
But your main backup would be your gallery representation.
The gallery and others allow you to take your mind off things they look after.
The time saved by you not doing those things would be huge.
But it's likely you don't do them and that has a negative effect on your career.
So they'd be helping you lift your game above its present levels.
You can focus totally on your painting and other things only you can do.

What if you spent a few minutes working out your ideal support team?
Just think of what sort of jobs someone could do to help your career along.
Even write a few lines about exactly what each job would entail.
You probably have some of these people already on your team.
Someone does your framing surely, and isn't there a gallery person (or two)?
There's someone who does all those other things listed above, it may be you.

Think of them (framer, gallery person,) as part of your support team.
Start using them that way by asking their advice on their specialty.
Take them into your confidence about your plans and ambitions.
Share everything with them and have regular meetings, even by phone!
Do what you'd do if they're employed by you and think about them like that.
They are your support people and when you are successful, they will be too.
Things you do for yourself treat them as if someone did them for you.
Write everything down then see if you can find people to do what you wrote.
They may only be part time (to start with).

Offer people incentives to be members of your team.
This may not be extra money, although that might be possible at some stage.
It could be simple things, like a free drawing for their birthday.
First opportunity to buy from each exhibition is another incentive worth trying.
An annual visit to your studio would be appreciated.

Eventually you will have your support team.
Most may be part time, and none actually on your pay-roll.
Keep having regular meetings and occasional social gatherings.
Then you too could strive for the artistic equivalent of an Olympic medal.
The longer your team stays together the better they should become.

You must also do the 'hard yards' just as the athlete does.
They rise early and train dedicatedly and also work at their game constantly.
They make sacrifices to be professional you must too.
Like the Olympic athlete, an artist just can't do it on raw talent!

Many artists do have that and are still not successful.
They have no understanding of success and the attitude necessary.
Professionalism is required for success in any field, including that of an artist.

But, you don't have to do it on your own!
Build a support infrastructure so you have time to focus on what you do best.
Think once more of the scenario painted above for professional artists.
Do you see some new and challenging careers within the support team?
That happened in sport will happen in art too -perhaps already under way?

3. Take back responsibility.

You need to understand how everything fits together.
You have to know the dynamic of your marketplace.
Initially understand the field - or niche - that you operate in.
Then you want to expand your outlook with different ideas.
So force yourself to go to events and places outside the art industry.

When you have a problem, you need to get to the root of that problem.
Ask why this is a problem for only then can you solve it in a meaningful way.
Asking "why" gives you a better perspective on reality.
It helps you gain confidence you can overcome challenges and problems.

Think about the future.
Not in a fantasy way, but about what is going to happen in a very short term.
What you believe based on knowledge of what is seen in your market.
Also within your career what is going to happen in the short-term.
Start developing the habit of moving before you feel totally ready.
That doesn't mean impulsive but most people wait too long to take action.
A more successful career or make more money or better circumstances
But they don't take the actions that will get them what they want.
Because they're afraid they might fail or they don't know enough.

You have to move before you think you're totally ready.
You learn as you go as it's the only way to get the knowledge you need.
Move before you're ready for you have to be willing to bet on yourself.
But what if you are not willing to bet on yourself?
You need to understand what currently stops you and what needs to change!
What do you need to do to believe the best bet you can make is on yourself.

It's easy to rationalize your doubts, fears and conservative instincts.
It's safe to wait for better circumstances when the economy isn't so good.
The more you think about it, it's easier to believe it's fool-hardy to take risks.
Contact the gallery when the economy improves as they'll look for artists.
There will be times when you know more, have money or better prepared.
But ultimately, that's a dangerous mindset to have.
Because what it really means is you have a lack of confidence in yourself.
And the lack of confidence is going to carry over to when times are better.

The greatest inventions and advances in technology or business.
Generally come during tough times or from a negative economic perspective.
You can't wait for the stars to get perfectly aligned for it never happens.
Conquer fear so learn through progress, which is to move to action.

4. Why exhibit at a gallery?

Reviewed by: Chantel Barber – (Bartlett, Tennessee)
1. Why do you want to be in a gallery anyway?
2. Will you consign or sell?
3. Are contracts or agreements a good idea?
4. Are you prepared to negotiate?
5. How do you decide what gallery you want to be in?

1. Why do you want to be in a gallery anyway?

Do you want people to see your works?
Do you feel you are now good enough?
Do you think this is the next step you should take, like most artists think!

Perhaps you want to make money?
Well that's what commercial galleries do.
They sell artist's works so they and the artist make money.
And that's why you want to be there.

Public galleries just show works.
You do not want to be there if you are interested in a professional career.

But there are alternatives.
You could exhibit at art shows and you might even win an award as well.
Use FaceBook too and then email and newsletters can be sent to prospects.
You'll spend years in a co-op as most co-op people can't sell their own work.
So how can they sell yours?

You might be able to participate in annual Art Fairs.
Juried shows at an arts center might also be a possibility.
Maybe you could have a solo show at a local restaurant or resort?
Perhaps your work fits in with antique displays?

But you may be making a common mistake (like many other artists).
Do you expect the works to sell themselves – well they don't and can't.
Do your local galleries actually sell stuff?
Is it low priced local area focused work?
Trees are a popular subject in some areas because people go to see them.
Without those trees there would be many fewer visitors.

Do the people at any antique place sell artwork?
Many do and if so your stuff may not need to stand out.

In fact it might be better if it doesn't!
Then you become an artist the buyer discovered on their visit to your area.
Charge more (much more) and paint smaller for then they are not souvenirs.
Just hanging artworks up somewhere in front of people doesn't sell anything.
People buy.
They buy for their own reasons not the reasons the seller thinks they should.
You and all the other artists need someone helping people buy.

Only a commercial gallery has a sales focus.
Even then many do not know exactly what to do.
Selling is finding out what people want to buy.
Then providing something that meets those requirements.

Even your presence may not be enough if you are not doing that.
That's because most artists just answer questions.
You should ask questions and listening carefully to the answers instead.
Anyone who does that can sell anything.

Artists rarely buy artworks.
People mainly buy because they are **NOT** artists.
They do not understand the mystery of creation so a work seems like magic.
To sell you need to preserve this mystery so do **NOT** answer questions.
At least not about the works and how they were done.
Gallery people where you consider consigning works should do the same.

But paint whatever you like.
How you actually do your work (collage etc.) is not related to sales.
What it looks like is.

So what is the very best way to make money?
Have a sell-out exhibition!
Then follow it up with another one.
Have you seen any sell out exhibitions?
Were they at a gallery and if so what kind of gallery were they at?

2. Will you consign or sell?

You should not begrudge your gallery making money.
They must live somehow and only make money selling artworks profitably.
Your task is to help them make money by selling your artworks.
Naturally this should be done in such a way that you make money too.
This is the essence of a successful business relationship.

The most usual form of selling in the art world is consigning work.
A gallery, art-show, dealer or selling organization places your work on sale.
They do whatever is necessary to attract buyers.
When the work is sold you are paid for the sale.
A commission is retained by the seller for their work on your behalf.
A commission is a % of the selling price but it may be an agreed amount.

This is NOT the most usual form of selling in the 'real' business world.
There the seller (retailer) buys stock from a manufacturer (wholesaler).
A seller pays the wholesale price and sells the goods for whatever they get.
Sellers of luxury items such as jewellery, have mark-ups of 150%.
They need this sort of margin to make money (naturally).
They also need to cover the many pieces that don't sell.
That's why they can have sales, where the reductions are quite large.
They still make a small profit, or at least get their money back.
Furniture and clothing retailers operate on a similar basis.

Most reproduction prints are sold this way too.
The publisher (wholesaler) sells to the picture framer (retailer).
They in turn sell the prints for whatever they can get.
When you consign work to a gallery, art-show or dealer you are taking a risk.
It is a greater risk than if you sold the work outright to them.
For they may not pay, they could lose your work or it may become damaged.
It cannot be sold elsewhere whilst it's at that outlet.

You deserve a higher return as an insurance against these possibilities.
BUT if they buy they deserve a greater reward than for commission sales.
They now take the greater risk for their money is invested in the work.
So you should recognize this in the transaction.
Gallery commission is 33.3% they might purchase work for 50% of sale price.
It is even likely that 50% will not be sufficient inducement.
You could exchange unsold works for ones of the same or greater value.

Artists sell from their own studio or gallery, and they are the only artist.
Frequently they have no choice, other than to take this path.

BUT before selling from your studio and at galleries, think carefully.
Selling outright to a gallery or dealer is **NOT** the same as selling to a client.
The former is a wholesale transaction, the latter is at the retail level.
A gallery is likely to generate many sales, the client only one (probably).
This is the same as a manufacturer sells direct from a factory or warehouse.
You're a retailer and do things a retail seller would do to attract buyers.

YOU should receive payment for this.
It's the share taken by the gallery, art show, or dealer for the same work.

Will you give a client a discount for sales at your studio?
If you do it is unlikely they will ever again buy your work from a gallery.
If this doesn't worry you don't be surprised if the gallery stops promoting you.
They really can't compete.
You offer lower price, latest works, better choice and can meet the artist.
Many artists realize this and do not sell from their studio.
Instead they refer potential clients to the most appropriate gallery.

If you must, or choose to, sell from your studio.
Any sales should be at the usual retail price or higher.
Preferably you charge **MORE** than the gallery price.
You offer better choice, opportunity to meet the artist and to see your studio.
The client should pay for these additional benefits.
You are entitled to whatever you can earn from them.
You won't undermine gallery pricing structure, which takes years to establish.

There's another reason you should ask a higher than usual retail price.
You preserve your gallery outlets loyalties for you are not competing.
Supply name and address to the gallery nearest where the client lives.
You'll be rewarded by the gallery, for loyalty gets loyalty in return.
Also pay the usual commission to the appropriate gallery (nearest the client).
If you do this, you'll be way ahead of other artists who supply that gallery.
A few dollars foregone may be a worthwhile long-term investment.
But do keep the margin you charged above the usual retail price.
This was for those extra benefits you provided.

3. Are contracts or agreements a good idea?

The main advantage of a contract is prevent later misunderstandings.
If necessary, you have them at the beginning whilst goodwill exists.
If there is something you don't like, argue for deletion, or amendment.
You can accept these things too, if everything else is satisfactory.
Negotiating early is way better than trying to sort something out much later.
Offering a contract facilitates clearing up potential misunderstandings.
Often a problem is something that needs explaining and expressing clearly.

Many artists feel uncomfortable about written contracts.
Consequently their agreements are of a handshake variety.
This is fine if you **REALLY** understand what is required and expected of you.
AND the gallery understands what you expect of them, but, do you?

It helps if a contract is at least offered.
It should set out the arrangements you have with your gallery for example.
It should take into account your needs and expectations as well.
But do you really understand a gallery's expectations?
The time for a discussion is on the first occasion you enter into negotiations.
You should have a reasonable discussion about what they expect of you.
That should be done **BEFORE** you consider bringing paintings to the gallery.
What sorts of paintings do they expect, what sizes, and in what price ranges?
Who is responsible for pricing anyway (they may assume it's their role)?
Who pays for any freight, either to or from the gallery?
What do they expect in the way of framing?
How often will they want a supply of fresh stock and how many works is this?

Does the gallery really understand your expectations?
A thing that need to be covered include the obvious one, commission rates.
However, you should also find out how soon you'll be paid following a sale.
What will happen when a client is paying off a work?
If you have an exhibition will there be charges in addition to the commission?
What will they be, and how much will they be expressed in $?
How do they plan to sell your works if they are not in an exhibition?
How long will the works stay there?
Just ask about anything you want to know!
What sort of support will they want from you?
This might be written material or your presence at some gallery functions.
What will be their view on you selling works from your studio?
Do not assume this will be OK, as in many cases it's not!

Assuming is a process that often leads to later problems.
Don't assume a gallery means what you think they do.
Ask them what is meant exactly, even if you think you know.
There is deception and malpractice for galleries are as honest as artists.
Most friction is from misunderstanding answers to the questions suggested.
It is really dumb not to ask dumb questions!
What else could you need agreements for?
It's not just galleries or agents, where contracts or agreements are useful.
Use them for commissions, models, for workshops with other organizations.

What records do you need?
You could have computerized stack sheets, as many artists' now-days do.
However a simple system is to have a delivery book, bought at a newsagent.
List artworks left, with their prices, the name of the gallery and the date.
Write any other special conditions, and have the gallery owner sign the page.
Issue the original and keep a carbon copy in your delivery book.

They may also give you a consignment note.
This is similar document, but issued by the gallery to you.
There should be an exchange of signed paper documentation.
This accompanies the handing over of the artworks.
Exactly the same thing applies with your agent (even if it's your spouse).

What basic information is required?
Most agreements need names and addresses, as well as signature and date.
They are for the parties making the agreement, as well any witnesses.
The timeframe of the agreement could also be included.
Penalties for lost or damaged stock, failure to meet deadlines, are noted.
These can be expressed in simple English (or your own language).
There is no need for a formal legal document although it will be legal
Bankruptcy is not unknown in artistic circles.
Often assets can be seized, and this might include your paintings.
You might have to prove ownership which a consignment note would do.

4. Are you prepared to negotiate?

When selling their works, many artists are not prepared to negotiate.
Often this is because someone else is doing the selling on their behalf.
And those people aren't willing to, or haven't the authority to, negotiate.
Yet all these same people negotiate with cars.
Also electrical goods, furniture, tyres, a house, or many other common items.
In everyday affairs it's fairly normal to negotiate a price.
Nobody expects to pay the asking price selling or buying a house.
We set fixed prices on artworks and resent potential clients who negotiate.

Why should someone obtain a reduction just because they ask?
However it is possible to increase value without reducing price.
Reduced price is what it is about gaining value.
Negotiating is about both buyer and seller gaining value.
Negotiating happens when someone has something the other person wants.
Both are prepared to bargain for it.
It isn't just in buying and selling, although that's what we'll consider here.
Negotiating is resolving any issue between two people, or groups of people.

Perhaps you should first consider whether you will negotiate or not?
Do you feel comfortable negotiating, generally or on a particular occasion?
If you don't want to, then there is no negotiation.
If you're uncomfortable you'll not be happy with an outcome from negotiation.
The other person buys on your terms and sales take place on this basis.

Will you get what you want from the negotiation?
If you don't then you've lost and would be better by not negotiating at all.
Weigh up whether is it better to sell at a lower than desired price.
Or not sell at all although only you can decide.
In markets where bargaining is normal a seller starts with a high.
There's room for reduction and still get what the seller wants, or better!
So if your price contains a margin for negotiating.
You are more likely to obtain a satisfactory price outcome from that process.

Negotiating takes time.
I have been negotiating the purchase of a car for some months now.
A potential buyer, the longer I take the more likely the seller loses patience.
Then they may accept an eventual lower offer.
There is a risk someone else comes along in the meantime and buys the car.
It can be worth the effort and time to negotiate on the sale of a car or house.
Thousands of dollars can be saved or gained.
How much effort is it worth to bargain on the sale of one of your paintings?

At what point in the sales cycle are you at with the work considered?
A fresh work, not yet placed on sale, you may be less inclined to negotiate.
If the work being considered has been in four exhibitions and six years old?
At some point we need to move on those works that hang around.
They thus become likely contenders for a bargain hunter.
Decide under what circumstances you'd be willing to negotiate.

How are your negotiation skills anyway?
Often artists find it difficult when confronted with a negotiation situation.
You have your paintings for sale and the prices are clearly marked.
Someone makes you an offer, which is less than the marked price.
They believe a marked figure is a starting point for negotiating on price.
You feel uncomfortable, because you are unprepared for such a situation.
You expected people to pay the money, if they want the work.
If you're prepared you've a chance to negotiate to advantage.

Provide support for your catalogue price.
Then you'll have a better chance of receiving that money from the negotiator.
If your position is backed by logic or precedent, you'll be in a better position.
It is priced the same as other works sold similar in size and subject matter.
The marked price includes a guarantee and reduction means you take it off.
Or it might be the copyright that is included, but deducted for any lesser sum.
Ask the negotiator what they offer you in return for the lower price.
In some cases this could even lead to a pleasant surprise.

Before a price reduction, there should be something given, or foregone.
For example you could sell at a reduced price works which you no longer do.
Rather than a newer work which is an important part of your artistic focus.

5. How do you decide what gallery you want to be in?

The type of gallery you need sell works like yours for high prices.
They have been in business for a long time with the same family ownership.
Artists have been there a long time (or are dead).
They are in the gallery district of big city and hold regular sell out exhibitions.
Will there be any problems?
They will not want you or your works for they already have enough artists.
They will not see your work as contributing to their bottom line.

Does the gallery earn a good commission?
Expect to pay a high commission, say 60% of selling price as a minimum.
Don't waste your time on any gallery only charging 25% to 40%.
They'll never earn the money you want and probably go out of business.
Without money they simply can't afford to promote their artists properly.
Generally the galleries with higher commission rates also sell best.
Or they sell at higher prices.
Your return can be better than a poor selling outlet with low commission.
Basically 0% of $0 is nothing, whereas 90% of $some is something.
It's your total dollar return that's most important to you.
It's certainly important in helping you calculate your likely income.

By deducting the commission you calculate a cost or wholesale price.
This may be important to help you decide which work to allocate to a gallery.
It's unlikely prints supplied at a high commission rate will give a good return.
Unless sold in great numbers.
So you should NOT price according to the commission structure.
Price according to what a buyer pays as this decides if the buyer buys.
They don't know about commission arrangements and don't care either.
It's actually none of their business.
Galleries with higher commission rates sell more works for more dollars.
Generally the galleries with the lower rate are looking for artists.

But how quickly will you be paid?
Although not a cost, speed of payment following a sale is important.
Generally if you're paid in the month following a sale it's quite reasonable.
The gallery does their books at the end of the month and pays artists then.
Anything longer than this is unusual.

It's uncommon for there to be other charges, except with an exhibition.
Then a gallery spends more money on your behalf than at other times.
Galleries take commissions, fees, or amounts you owe from sales payments.

This seems to suit artists too.
Sometimes a gallery will take a work instead of collecting money for a debt.
This is a good arrangement for artists, although these days it's less common.

What about time payment?
Less obvious but necessary, is how are you paid if a client pays off a work.
The best arrangement is they pay you as for an outright sale.
The worst arrangement is they pay you nothing until all money is collected.
A reasonable arrangement is you receive money as paid by the customer.
If you've been paid your share, then the gallery collects its part of the sale.
Freight is a cost when exhibiting at a gallery and also elsewhere too.
Moving a whole exhibition, including larger works, cannot be done cheaply.
Works tend to stay longer at a gallery.
The total freight may be less than if supplying art shows every other week.
Relate total freight to total sales to make cost comparisons.

Most artists are looking for that new golden buyer/supporter/collector.
Past purchasers are the more likely to buy again.
They are likely to buy from where they bought previously too.
One artist has been selling through galleries since 1967 with some success.
His main mistake is not collecting names, addresses and email addresses.
A successful gallery has all this plus aggressiveness to go for more business.

Eventually the best galleries for your career are those you already have.
You know where they are and you know how they work.
Your best return on investment is to spend time building those relationships.
Those galleries know and trust the people they have dealt with before.
You are not a stranger to them.
Provided you have treated them well they're likely to stick with you.
Loyalty gets loyalty!
That's why it is worth taking time and care when first starting your gallery search.
That's the time to make sure you have made the right choice!
The repercussions of a wrong decision will last a long time.

How do you decide who are those special galleries?
America researchers found 5% of households buy 85% of Levi jeans sold.
They also found that 8% of US households buy 84% of the Diet Coke sold.
21% percent of American moviegoers represent 80% of total attendance.
An Australian bank found 8% of its clients contribute 125% of profit.

These figures are true of every business including galleries.
Some people are big users of a product / service but others aren't.
Some people are easy to sell to and spend up big.

Others are always causing more work for you and spend the least.
You'll have seen this yourself - are other artists good clients?

You'll find around 20% of your galleries generate 80% of your turnover.
You've read in the papers or seen on TV, about casinos and the high rollers.
The high rollers are a few clients who provide most of the casino income.
As this income is huge it stands to reason the casino should do them favours.

The best galleries have clients like these.
So once you are on their team contact your best galleries often.
It's a good investment if you provide reasons for them to remember you.
You will be top of mind when they plan something new.

The hard part is getting established in the first place.
Just focus on one thing at a time in the beginning.
There is a bonus for those artists who can identify their best outlets.
Similarities between best clients, things they share, suburbs or professions.
This knowledge will be helpful when talking to other galleries.

5. What can galleries do?

Reviewed by Pauline Adair – (Sunshine Coast, Queensland)

1. Do you have a long term vision about your career?
2. So what is your target gallery like?
3. Consider your potential relationship with a prospective gallery.
4. What is the artist gallery relationship about?
5. Finding the right gallery.
6. Finalizing the gallery deal.
7. Will a gallery guard the value perception of your works?
8. I assume you are interested in making money as an artist.

1. Do you have a long term vision about your career?

Most artists tend to focus on an individual painting.
An exhibition is a collection of their paintings.
Exhibitions can generate an ever-increasing income spiral.
Start right and upward income spiral can go for the duration of your career.
What if the focus is on the exhibition, as one of a series of exhibitions?
Then there's a different mind-set.
A career can be an ongoing stream of exhibitions.
Be pro-active about generating this income stream if you know what to do.
How you approach exhibitions can be an extension of this thinking.
Each exhibition builds on those that have gone before.
Each additional exhibition should generate a higher income at the next one.

That's why you should get the first one right.
Then your profit compounds as prices rise along with the additional sales.
Additional referrals increase the number of works you can sell.
Money earned from sell-out exhibitions is additional to what you earn now!
You are the professional artist running your business.
There is very little to be gained by **MERELY READING** what I write.
To get **ANY** benefit you must actually **DO** something!

There will always be artists who want gallery representation.
There's not really anything wrong with that.
A top gallery can earn you sales that would not otherwise come your way.
It's just that becoming one of a gallery's artists is not that easy!
Particularly if they are well established.
These galleries already have a team of artists to whom they give their loyalty.
To break into this scene is going to be difficult but here are a few ideas.
Visit as many galleries as you can.
They have different styles and objectives.

Get a feel for what they exhibit and how they do things.
Where the gallery is situated tells you something about likely clientele.
For example they may be in a tourist precinct.
The gallery owner's personality is also likely to play a big part in how it is run.
Try to assess these things in relation to your work and your ambitions.

Aim at having work in more than one gallery.
There's a hierarchy of galleries - some are prestigious, and others modest.
You may need to work your way up the ladder.
Find out what it is going to cost you to exhibit.
There are things involved in an exhibition which you may have to pay for.
Publicity, wine, glasses, food, invitations, photography, postage, commission.
Framing, flowers and "thank you" notes are some other expenses.
Different galleries have different policies so don't be surprised at variations.
Just make sure you know what you might be up for.

2. So what is your target gallery like?

The best galleries are business-like.
They are to make money for themselves and they make money for artists.
So is a gallery just like any other kind of business - well they should be!
No gallery can make money by selling cheap artworks.
Your works should be a good-quality product that's at reasonably priced.
Their clients should be interested in what you do now and in the future too.
A gallery is just as concerned with the future as the present.

But works might be displayed after they are sold (with a red spot).
A gallery director knows where it belongs so they can obtain more sales.
A gallery can sell more than a work to a client but it is not easy at the start.
Eventually the same people return regularly for paintings and commissions.

They are only successful if they appeal to a focused niche market.
Your gallery should target people who are trying to solve similar problems.
Do your works solve that problem, if not then that's not a gallery for you?
There's no point trying to sell art nobody at that gallery wants.
A gallery can't make miracles so if you think that they will and should!
Knowing clients to seek, is critical to success in a business including yours.
There is no future dealing with the wrong prospects!
There's no future in a gallery that attracts the wrong people for you either!
The best business is in response to the needs of a specific niche market!

Your gallery should be one that attracts people in your target market.
Which groups of people are most likely to buy what you do?
For example my website (when I had one) was directly to professional artists.
NO attempt to cater for hobby artists, academics or those interested in art.
Just those who wished to make money from their artistic activity.
Your strategies should aim at galleries rather than clients and prospects.
The **RIGHT** gallery can access potential buyers for your works.
They also have knowledge so the potential buyers become actual buyers.
Which means they can also obtain more sales?
A gallery can sell more than one work to a client.
So could you but it would be more difficult.

When you consider joining a gallery you will check out their reputation.
They should offer good client service and be very professional at all times.
Offend clients by referring them to a gallery who treats them poorly?
It's likely any potential gallery you talk to will think about you the same way!
Can they give honest sincere recommendations to their clients about you?
If they can't do this, then no gallery will offer you space on their walls.

Sincerity helps the selling process.
It's hard to recommend an artist if you don't like their work/.

So do your homework.
Visit a gallery, what do they do **AND** talk to other artists whose work you see.
Do these things **BEFORE** you show works or talk about yourself as an artist.

3. Consider your potential relationship with a prospective gallery.

You will be involved in an important negotiation.
If you haggle with a trader in Hong Kong it's unlikely either will meet again.
The relationship is one for the duration of the negotiation and that's it!
You might take a tough stance or the trader more willing to soften his view.
Once you move on he's not likely to see you so he must sell now or not at all.

But negotiating with your prospective gallery is different.
There's usually a desire for a long-term relationship.
Then it's a good idea to consider if your demands will affect the relationship.
You want excellent service for a considerable period.
Then your negotiating posture should be softer than with a trader.
If you value the potential relationship then you'll not negotiate to the limits.

With a gallery you may concede a little more than you'd ideally want.
A long term relationship is more important than the very best deal.

On the other hand if a prospective buyer wants a reduced price.
They show little respect for you as an artist or business-person.
Drive a hard negotiation with no concern for a relationship, there is none.

It very well might be that being rejected by a gallery is the norm.
But the reasons are really very practical, and logical.
Artists wanting to be in a gallery is **FAR** greater than openings available.
What if every artist who wanted to show in a gallery was able to?
The market would be flooded and the gallery system would lose credibility.
Works would be average, mediocre, and non-remarkable.
Galleries act somewhat like a filter.
There are many artists who want to be accepted but rejections are inevitable.
As in other areas of human interaction sometimes you meet rude people.

But sometimes this happens.
A successful gallery sold work regularly and then changed hands.
The new owners were farmers!
They thought running a gallery would be nice for their retirement!
So they took on every artist who walked through their doors.
The gallery was messy and unprofessional so the good artists pulled out.
The gallery closed down.

One artist experienced the opposite though.
His gallery encounter underlined just how generous some galleries can be.

But it also involved rejection.
Richard Bruland (Los Angeles) wanted an outlet in the Pacific Northwest.
He asked a collector if he knew a gallery that might be interested in his work.
The collector had just bought work from a gallery in Portland, Oregon.
He would contact them and recommend they have a look at Richard's work.

This is the type of introduction artists dream of!
Richard called the gallery, and they agreed to see his work.
He made an appointment, and drove from L.A. to Portland a few weeks later.
Jane Beebe, the owner, really liked what Richard showed her.
But she didn't feel it was quite the right 'fit' for her gallery.

But then what she did shocked Richard.
She said "well, you're here in Portland - let's see what we can do".
Jane picked up the phone, and called several very good galleries.
She told their directors she was coming right over with an artist from L.A.
Jayne also said they should consider his work.
She personally walked him to those galleries and introduced Richard.

Richard's comment:
Amazing, and I've never forgotten that kindness.
I know that seldom happens, but it did to me.

4. What is the artist gallery relationship about?

How do art galleries work?
For many artists, this is one of the mysteries of life.
If they understood they'd be able to approach a gallery with more confidence.
One of the problems for many artists is they have blinkers on.
They're totally focused on their own work.
They don't go out to find new Galleries to represent them.
They are too focused on creating and trust that eventually the works will sell!!

Now this is necessary, or you wouldn't create anything.
But it can lead you into thinking everyone else has the same point of view.
Well they simply can't and don't.
No-one else can have your kind of understandings about your work.
You know the hours you've spent creating it.
You know the blind alleys you travelled before the work was finished.
An artist carted her art around for two years as she commenced trying to sell.
She went into every group exhibition going, won prizes, but didn't sell.
Probably the prizes were her last hope, and kept her going.

You know how it went from blank canvas to finished and framed, work.
You know thoughts and feelings as you paint early works leading to this one.
You know more than I've suggested about your work, for you are the creator.
A spectator, maybe a potential buyer, or even me, can look at your work.
We can guess at those things, particularly if we happen to paint ourselves.
We may think of other paintings by you, or other artists, and note similarities.
We might even think about your colours and if they'll match the curtains!
We always relate our thoughts to our experiences, as we look at your work.
Observers start with a finished work and then relates that to his experience.
Only you have the experience of creating the work, it's your start point.
The gallery owner is also an observer in relation to you and your work.

For the gallery owner, the gallery is their creative work.
They are creators, and you an occasional visitor viewing their work, a gallery.
Your expectation of galleries is made up of visits to this and other galleries.
Similarly their understanding is arrived at by looking at your works.
As well as those of other artists, and talking to you at the same time.

You need a clear idea of the relationship between a gallery and artists.
Confusion of roles and expectations gives problems to artists and galleries.
Most often that's because there are unrealistic expectations.
The relationship is essentially a business one.

It's about making money for both parties.
If neither artist nor gallery can make money, the relationship breaks down.
Often artists begrudge the gallery making money by selling their works.
But if they don't make money, how else can they continue to sell the works?
Both parties do what they do best and combine for mutual benefit.
If there's no mutual benefit, then one party is being taken advantage of.
Let's have a closer look at what the essential responsibilities are.

An artist is primarily responsible for the creation of artworks.
A gallery is primarily responsible for marketing the artist and their artworks.
Either can give advice and suggestions to the other in their responsibility.
BUT creative decisions are the artist and marketing decisions by the gallery.
Obviously what one does affects the other, so there's value in co-operation.
BUT someone has to make decisions or nothing happens.

There could be problems!
An artist can present works to a gallery that the gallery finds hard to market.
Perhaps a new style different from earlier works or inappropriate price range.
Or a gallery may market in a way the artist feels is unsuited for their work.
Perhaps they don't place ads in the local newspaper.

If what one party does is intolerable, the second has a right of veto.
The business arrangement ends.
An artist continually supplies what the gallery considers inappropriate work.
The gallery can just stop exhibiting that artist and their work.
But if the best efforts of the gallery to market an artist have failed.
Then an artist can withdraw their works from that gallery.
If a veto is exercised there is no longer an artist and gallery relationship.
The relationship outlined gives each party freedom and also responsibility.
In the area in which they can reasonably be expected to have expertise.
Their combined efforts are geared towards making money for both.

Art galleries work by marketing artists and artworks to make money.
They do not exist to provide wall space for an artist to show their work.
The walls are tools to be used for the money making process.
If you can help the gallery do its job, then rewards will flow your way.
Understand the gallery approach and you'll be able to see where you can fit.
Opportunities to exhibit follow this kind of thinking.

You might think a gallery should promote your work on TV.
OR by printing coloured brochures featuring ten of your works.
These are things that are likely to increase chances of selling your work.

But remember the object is to make a profit, for you and for the gallery.
Your idea costs $5,000 to implement, the gallery is on a 33.3% commission.
Perhaps you have $24,000 worth of paintings on the wall in the exhibition?
They usually sell 2/3 of your paintings.
Without special promotion the gallery could receive $5,333 (1/3 of $16,000).
If **ALL** sell with a special promotion, they spend $5000 for an extra $2,667!
This is a pretty big ask.

Now work out the situation if they usually sell 50% or perhaps 25%.
What if your exhibition is worth $10,000 or if your works add up to $150,000.
Then the extra $5,000 will be well spent, even if only 25% are usually sold.
In this analysis I'm assuming your prices are realistic rather than optimistic.
You could also calculate your own benefit from the extra $5,000 promotion.
Work out a proposal where both you and the gallery benefit.
Worthwhile discussions are sure to follow.

Can you provide free promotional tools, tips and strategies?
You don't need to tell them how to do their job, but you can certainly help.
A professional artist provides all a gallery needs to be successful.
They should teach you everything you need to know to earn good money.
Success is mutually dependent.

5. Finding the right gallery.

There are many things to consider if looking for a gallery for your work.
Is it long established or newly emerging?
An established gallery will have a track record of success to stay in business.
This is more likely if the same people operated it for a considerable time.

The new gallery is more of a gamble.
It may or may not stay in business.
If it does and you are one of their artists you're a winner, if not you lose a lot.
Monitor the situation closely if you are in a gallery of only two or three years.

What kind of work do they sell?
Take a look at any prospective gallery to see whether your work would fit in.
Most galleries tend to specialise and that's likely what they sell best too.
If your work is an 'orphan' style your sales may be few and far between.
Look at the price range of the works on show - is yours much the same?
If yours is too different, either cheaper or dearer sales might be hard.
Is the layout and appearance of the gallery professional?
This doesn't mean expensive but they should work well and look efficient.

How does a prospective gallery promote their artists?
In particular how would they promote work such as yours?
Merely hanging your work on a wall is a start, but that's all it is.
You should get much more than this from a good gallery.

What are their people like?
Are they competent, keen, knowledgeable – how do they deal with clients?
If you can, talk to some of their clients to see what their view of the gallery is.
Taking all this into account your work should fit the gallery's target market.
Don't be disappointed if you don't, just move on elsewhere.
When you find a suitable gallery what's the best way to approach it?
Well the first thing to do is make sure you really are ready for this step.
Gallery visitors have long memories.
Their first impressions will be the ones that are strongest and stay with them.
It will not matter what you do, years later which is tough but that's how it is.

But your work is excellent, and you're quite confident.
Visit galleries you'd like to have your work in – friends to check them out too.
Gallery people believe they can spot an artist a mile off.
So dress more like a client when you make your visit.
Talk to their people about the gallery as if you are a possible client.

See how they deal with potential clients (which you are at this stage).
Ask about artists who paint a bit like you do - what sorts of work is on show?
What kind of policy does the gallery seem to have about the work it shows?
Can people pay off works?
Is there any guarantee?
Is your work compatible with these?

That's the easy part, unless you live 400 km from the nearest gallery.
If you do live a long way from your preferred outlets, there's really no choice.
You travel there, at least initially but perhaps, later on they'll come to you.

The hard part is to find out about the financial state of the gallery.
Are they selling works reasonably well?
Do they pay their artists promptly?
You learn this from experience and then it will become very important to you.
One artist had this happen when she hadn't been paid for about 3 months.
Finally she went in to enquire about her money
But the gallery had packed up and gone, and she never was paid.

How long they've been in business is a guide.
If they survive many years will be by selling works and paying artists.
This particularly applies if it's been the same people for that period.
Be very cautious about becoming involved with a new gallery.
Similarly avoid one that's changed hands regularly.
A sound financial background or past gallery experience could be OK.
This doesn't mean all old and established galleries are perfect either.
BUT they are more likely to continue.

Find out some of the artists who exhibit at these galleries.
Telephone them and ask what the gallery is like, how often they exhibit, etc.
In other words find out as much as possible about the gallery.
BEFORE you start talking to the owner about yourself and your work.
As a result of research eliminate some but others come to your notice.

This phase is worth spending time on, and most artists don't do it.
You are going to make a commitment to a gallery.
You owe it to yourself to ensure it's a gallery you are with, in ten years' time.
It's a first step in a long-term relationship that should be mutually rewarding.

6. Finalizing the gallery deal.

You'll probably be concerned about what a gallery will do for you.
You should have your expectations and ascertain whether they can be met.
But you must also be realistic.
For instance you may have to commence at lower prices than you expected.
If sales come the gallery will be just as eager as you to see your prices rise.
You may be asked to supply works for stock before an exhibition is offered.
Even then it may be shared with someone else, not ideal but common.
Find out as much as possible about what they'll do for you.

What can you do for them?
Many artists do not consider this aspect, supplying the work is sufficient.
You should consider this if you want to stand out from the crowd.
Doing so, you indicate a willingness to be a partner in a commercial venture.
Your relationship with the gallery is not a serf and master, nor vice versa.
Ensure a regular supply of your best work in price ranges of their choice.
Supply as much supporting material as you can to help your promotion.
Get in the gallery's good books a list of people interested in your work.

Don't forget the financial considerations?
Try to sort these matters out right at the start.

Negotiate points you don't like, get explained if you don't understand.
You need to know commission rates and how quickly you're paid after a sale.
How will you be paid if a client pays off a work and are there extra charges?
A cause of friction is who pays for what and how it is levied.
Let's look at commission rates.
If a gallery sells on consignment there's a commission levied on each sale.
This is an amount they earn by doing things to sell your work.
It is also to cover those things they do to generally sell art works.

Remember too they have to do things even if your work doesn't sell.
It's the gallery's share of the sale which they have earned.
Don't begrudge them this, for without it they can't exist at all.
33.3% rate is minimum, 40% common and major galleries have higher rates.
Less than the minimum and the gallery will probably go out of business.
Unless they are turning over huge volumes of works.
So be very wary of a low commission rate, even 33.3% can be difficult.
The more the gallery does for you, a higher commission rate can be justified.

Look for value for money, not just cheapness.
It's better to pay 60% of some sales than 25% on no sales.

You can always adjust your prices upwards in the 50% situation.
You can start on 65% and after an agreed number of sales the rate is 60%.
Negotiate an even lower figure when your sales credibility is established.

Does the gallery pass on costs?
When an exhibition is held, there are costs associated with social functions.
Food, drink, postage, printing, and music all add up and someone has to pay.
This is an area of friction between an artist and a gallery, but easy to avoid.

It's common to charge artists for these expenses, or for a share (50%).
You will not have any idea what this cost is in real money.
Usually an amount is deducted for your share from the sales,
Later on you can get quite a surprise at what this all adds up to.
Then you may feel the gallery was free spending at your expense.
So don't agree to this kind of thing.
Although some galleries do not change an artist at all for opening expenses.

It's not necessarily wrong to have you share some of the costs.
BUT you should know what they are beforehand and in actual money.
Ask the gallery for a budget which shouldn't be hard as they do regularly.
Then you can agree to meet some or all to the amounts in the budget.

Another approach, some galleries use, is to charge an exhibition fee.
This is a set amount towards the costs associated with an exhibition.
It may be $50, $100, $500 or whatever amount the gallery determines.
BUT you'll know what you are up for beforehand.
As your sales rise you may be able to negotiate this fee downwards.
Galleries take commissions, fees, or whatever you may owe, from sales.
Some even take works for money owed a tradition going back years.
It's better for you as a work hasn't cost you $ value it is exchanged for!
But this value is something that should be agreed upon beforehand.
Should this be retail price (not really) or wholesale price (possibly)?
Whatever it is, you should know.

What arrangements will there be when a work is paid off?
You should be paid before a client takes delivery as it's still yours.
You should get paid before the gallery receives its total share too.
You may be paid in a series of payments or just one sum.

Ask questions!
If you're not sure of anything, ask questions, don't worry about being dumb.
Nothing is dumber than **NOT** asking questions you pay for ignorance later.
Generally you should try to obtain as much information as you can.

This helps decide if you'll join this gallery if the opportunity is offered.
You'll be able to deal more effectively with other galleries too.
Find out when they will be letting you know the results of your discussion.
Often it's straight away, but not always.
If they offer a spot in their team, it's a good idea to get time to think about it.
It might not matter if every aspect is not as you would prefer.
But the major factors should be and if they are not, decline the offer.

7. Will a gallery guard the value perception of your works?

It's a perception that is very fragile and easily damaged.
Each work is something like a piece of porcelain tea set.
Once one piece is damaged; all are lessened in value.
I'm not talking about actual physical damage but perceived value damage.

A lesser work reduces value of all works if client attitude is changed.
Constantly be on your guard to maintain a high value perception at all times.
You can convey an appreciation of value for your works.
Framing is a key component in positioning your work in a gallery.
A frame can give a luxury image **BUT** it can make works appear cheap.
But that's not the only way to position your work in a gallery!

For example they warrant museum like care and they're precious.
When you show works to a gallery (or prospect) wear white cotton gloves.
Insist they are to be worn at all galleries handling your works.
All public gallery employees wear white cotton gloves when handling works.
So why not commercial galleries and even (or more so) art show organizers?
If you wish to follow the white gloves idea give them a pair of gloves.
This tells the gallery people you value your works and they should too.
The message is also conveyed to their (and your) clients.

Now what about if one of your galleries doesn't do this?
What happens if one of your buyers visits several galleries, as many do?
What do they think?
Well at least they'll think that gallery is a lesser gallery, as indeed it may be.
They think you do not enforce your standards or are not aware of the breach!
It's also likely they'll wonder why you have works there at all.
This can start to erode confidence in the value of your works.

Many leading artists don't show in what they deem lesser outlets.
It's not just they get fewer sales but to preserve perceived value of all works.
Having works for sale in lesser outlets tends to reduce value in better ones.
That's if their clients know - **BUT** it could increase value in the lesser outlets!

Some better galleries insist you do not show in lesser outlets!
Where would you rather sell at, a better outlet or a lesser one?
So you should take a great deal of care just what works you place where.
A lesser outlet can be very good for selling lesser works (if you do them).
Also sell works hard to move elsewhere (by reducing prices considerably).

Thus those galleries could become your wholesale outlets.
Focus on turning over stock to recover something.
You can use auctions this way too.
This strategy needs careful handling, some better galleries object to this too!
In the end the best outlets are valuable and worth keeping.

8. I assume you are interested in making money as an artist.

Major sales eventuate when exhibitions work.
So a sell-out exhibition is worth a special effort!
What will you paint ad what sizes and price will you have?
Exhibitions at a gallery can provide the best result.
BUT they should know what they are doing.
Just to make sure to ask what exactly that will be.

How can you make your exhibitions work?
Should you have a preview?
How can cultural leaders help you?
Are there things to know when selling your exhibition to the gallery?
Assume the worst but plan for the best result.

Could a journalist help?
An artist sent a journalist a very tiny watercolour from a life drawing session.
She loved it and wrote an article on a small exhibition at a home studio.
A photo was included and the exhibition was a sellout!

Don't forget to use your contact lists?
How will you make presentations count?
What are your responses to potential comments?
Accept them, sort them out and take on board those that help.

When does the selling stop?
If someone else can be better than you they are worth paying.
How can you or your agent sell more effectively?
What are the purchase signals shown by a prospect?
What is a presentation about?

If someone else can be better than you they are worth paying.
How can you or your agent sell more effectively?
What are the purchase signals shown by a prospect?
What is a presentation about?

How about a series of exhibitions at the gallery of your choice?
What do you have to do - could you kick-start your continuing career?
Understand the need for self-promotion so find out what else you can do?

An exhibition is an opportunity for bulk sales (sell the lot).
Don't waste this opportunity BUT most artists focus on getting more clients.
Let's just get more clients, get more clients, get more clients and we'll be OK.

But what about selling more stuff to existing clients?
Few people ever really take this step.
The focus is usually on getting more front-end clients.
But there's a goldmine waiting in your current client database.

Another way to get more sales is to sell people more stuff more often.
The easiest way to do this is to simply create more products.
Offer them to your clients on a regular scheduled basis (exhibitions).
Note the words "regular" and "scheduled".
The best way is to actually plan your new works for a year in advance.
If you put good stuff out, your clients are literally waiting for something new.
They wish you'd hurry up with another new work!
Artists think they saturate the market if they release new works regularly.
Just doesn't happen!
On the other hand you can save your new works for an exhibition.
Exhibitions are usually regular and scheduled.
AND you have the opportunity to sell the **LOT** in one go.

Selling is helping people buy.
There are characteristics necessary for a sell-out exhibition.
So if you are somewhat skeptical that's understandable.
BUT artists have successful exhibitions in various parts of the world.

It's not just luck as obviously something is done to make that happen.
Those exhibitions involved a broad range of artists, doing a variety of things.
They don't depend on a specific style of painting to identify you as an artist.
But there needs to be a correlation between what you do and how it's sold.

Confidence is a major requirement for a successful exhibition career.
Without confidence you will achieve little no matter how well you paint.
You can sell-out exhibitions if there is commitment and single-mindedness.
Any successful professional artist needs that!

Another key element is people willing to buy your work.
You may have those too.

A third ingredient is knowing exactly what to do.
Sales and marketing strategies major galleries normally provide.
Not all galleries do this for **MOST** do **NOT KNOW** what to do.
If you seek a new outlet for your work you must assume this is likely.

Exhibitions can be leveraged for major career momentum.
For example, sales at a well-known gallery are often quite public.

That can launch a continued successful and sustained artistic career.
This is not necessarily what most other artists say you should do.
BUT someone has to do it or you'll end up like all those other artists!

WHERE NEXT?

BUT being a professional artist is NOW harder than it ever was.
There are other books that link with this book.
You might need one or more of them:

PRICE RIGHT - Then sell.
http://www.amazon.com/dp/B087S85HS8

PLANNING - Means success.
http://www.amazon.com/dp/B087SCD1NY

CAREER BASICS - Planning.
http://www.amazon.com/dp/B087SCJYX3

FINDING BUYERS - How?
http://www.amazon.com/dp/B087SM58GJ

FIRST WEBSITE - Simple is best.
http://www.amazon.com/dp/B087SFZ6RD

SUCCESSFUL SELLING - Learn how.
http://www.amazon.com/dp/B088GDFNQK

FRAMING = helps sales
http://www.amazon.com/dp/B087SGS6MB

CHRISTMAS - Special approaches.
http://www.amazon.com/dp/B087SHDKPN

PRODUCTIVITY – the foundation
http://www.amazon.com/dp/B087S87HLD

COPYRIGHT - making money from copyright sales.
http://www.amazon.com/dp/B0892HWYTV

NOT NOW:

Perhaps one of these books could interest you then?

Write about your own memories.
http://www.amazon.com/dp/B087DWKPTP

A simple way to start developing creativity.
If you are a parent, teacher or someone who meets a group regularly?
http://www.amazon.com/dp/B088T1KFQZ

Here is how most people start becoming an artist!
http://www.amazon.com/dp/B088Y1DPL6

More of my memories.
http://www.amazon.com/dp/B088Y4RPL9

Start an art career but it's **NOW** is harder than it ever was.
http://www.amazon.com/dp/B088T7VJ76

SEND TO:

**Know anyone interested in chocolate recipes?
Then send them this link.**
http:/www.amazon.com/dp/B0882HK9Q9

Know anyone interested in THIS book?
http://www.amazon.com/dp/B08FP5NR3X

www.ingramcontent.com/pod-product-compliance
Lightning Source LLC
Chambersburg PA
CBHW020620220526
45463CB00006B/2630